Palmwine Sounds

Copyright © 2024 Palmwine Publishing Limited Nigeria

All rights reserved. No part of this publication may be reproduced, distributed, or transmitted in any form or by any means, including photocopying, recording, or other electronic or mechanical methods, without the prior written permission of the publisher, except in the case of brief quotations embodied in critical reviews and certain other non-commercial uses permitted by copyright law.
Author: Palmwine Sounds

Illustrations
Palmwine Sounds (inner)
Kehinde Omotosho (Cover)

ISBN (Paperback): 978-1-917267-18-2
ISBN (E-Book): 978-1-917267-19-9
Published by Nubian Republic on behalf of Nucifera Analysis Limited Nigeria, an imprint of Palmwine Publishing Nigeria.
Email: info@palmwinepublishing.com
Address (UK): 86-90 Paul Street, London EC2A 4NE
Address (Nigeria): 1A Jos Road, Bukuru, Plateau State, Nigeria.
www.palmwinepublishing.com
www.raffiapress.com
www.nuciferaanalysis.com

Sausage Union By Palmwine Sounds

Sausage Union

This will be a tale of sense and wisdom (Sense in Nigerian Pidgin English refers to someone who thinks they are smarter than everyone else). A third chapter in the sausage series, still set in the same warehouse in Leeds, West Yorkshire, but now focused on the union. It analyzes whether the union is performing its due diligence or is simply part of the warehouse, not fighting for the truths and rights that a union should. As usual, names won't be mentioned, but my story must be told.

Bari mu buga labari (Let's tell a story)

Tale of Sense and Wisdom
Sense feels smarter than wisdom
Like saying yawo, it surpasses cunning.
Wisdom is patient and steady,
Wisdom comes with time.
Sense only sees the moment,
Sense knows no game theory.

Sausage Union By Palmwine Sounds

The head union representative at the warehouse, from my perspective, has one foot in the union and another protecting the interests of the warehouses. I had to chase him for everything, from grievances to contacting other union representatives to help with my case. Some people at the warehouse told me at the start to find a different union, saying I wouldn't find justice with this one, but I didn't heed that advice.

Sausage Union By Palmwine Sounds

Zion or Babylon

There is no in-between in this battle.
You must pick a side and stand firm.
One foot is in the Babylonian kingdom,
The other tries to tread Zion's path,
Acting as Babylonians do, with manipulative ways.
Pick a side and show your true self.
My advice: tread the righteous side.

Sausage Union _{By Palmwine Sounds}

It took almost three weeks to get him to write my formal grievance. He accessed the investigation of my informal grievance, which he wasn't supposed to view without my permission. He tried to bury wickedness to protect the warehouse's interests, telling my Hallelujah stories. He claimed the union would file a grievance against Mr. U because of so many complaints—something unheard of, while being supported by the manager who always played ignorant, telling me, "He's a good guy." Maybe he is to you. I also had to chase him for contacts of other union representatives, but eventually gave up and got them from the union's webpage.

Hallelujah Stories

I can turn blue into black or red.
I can change the colors of the rainbow.
Inspiritus heavenus (speaking in tongues).
Babylonians have no truth in them,
Twisting stories to bury the truth.
Jah's children will always see through.

Sausage Union   By Palmwine Sounds

I know myself. If I have a goal, I won't stop until I get what I want. All I want is for truth and justice to prevail. Your job comes with a badge for social justice, but you have stained that. Even the warehouse HR doesn't perform its role effectively. They picked the word "polygamy" from a poetry book titled God Bless Women to paint me as sexualizing women—a very colonial or imperial mentality, which I could call

Sausage Union
By Palmwine Sounds

racism from my viewpoint. They sent documents to everyone but me. Am I being looked down on because I am African? Most, if not all, of upper management is British. They're clearly conducting investigations to get me out of the company for pointing out issues in the factory. Maybe they're protecting British interests. HR doesn't support me until I email upper management. Maybe they're working with the union.

Social Justice

I am Rasta,
Social justice is woven into my DNA.
Built on truth,
Fighting for rights,
The last truth of creation.
Union representative,
Human resources,
Dealing with Babylonians,
Take off that badge.
You insult it,
Spitting on those
Who came before you.

Sausage Union By Palmwine Sounds

What pains me even more is him ignoring phone calls, promising to call me back but never delivering. Imagine if it wasn't me. Most people would give up, receive no support, and leave the factory. Even a manager told me, after my informal grievance, "If you want to leave, you can leave." The union representative said the same thing. How many times has this game been played? If there's no support, why

# Sausage Union By Palmwine Sounds

fight? But I won't give up. No gree (Don't agree) for anyone. He stayed back with a manager to discuss after meetings—discussing what, I don't know.

No gree

I'm stubborn, I know,
I will find a way.
No is another's yes.
Aggressively, I'll find a way.
I know I'm right.
Babylon will fall.

Sausage Union _{By Palmwine Sounds}

I had to brush up on employment laws and get advice from legal aid. If I hadn't known about the protected act, Babylon could have won. But Jah guides and protects. I even had to file a complaint against the head union representative for not performing due diligence in his role.

Just Trust

The faith of a mustard seed
Can move mountains.
Imagine the faith of a mountain,
That can move the universe.
When the universe aligns,
Sense is just digging its hole.

I am a soldier of Jah, a knight in his army.
Jah Soldier
Put on my helmet,
Which are my locks.
My words
Become lightning.
My eternal mission

Sausage Union
By Palmwine Sounds

Is to destroy Babylon,
To fight for truth and rights,
And to destroy the hopes of the wicked,
Until Zion's gates call me,
This Rasta man shall tread on.

Sausage Union
By Palmwine Sounds

This is my unbiased analysis. Let's focus on the positives.

One thing I can say is that the women in the union that I've had the opportunity to interact with are all very supportive and go far beyond to help.

Women

They always stand for right,
They always fight for right.
Hearts of silver and gold,
Social justice in their DNA.
Men create problems,
Expecting women to fix them.
Always standing for truth and rights.
God, bless all women fighters.

Sausage Union By Palmwine Sounds

The union representative who handles my appeals was supportive at first, but these days he's getting cold feet, even going as far as to tell me to just let it go. Me? You must be joking. Stand firm. He ignores my phone calls until I contact those above him.

Sausage Union
By Palmwine Sounds

Babylon Ways

Babylon's ways are different.
Don't try to understand.
Just strike them with a cane.
Ignite the cane with flames,
To cause maximum damage.

There is no rest for the wicked. Babylon shall pay.

Sausage Union By Palmwine Sounds

No Rest

The wicked do not rest,
So why should I, as Rasta?
It's not possible.
I shall work double,
Until my goal is met,

Sausage Union By Palmwine Sounds

Treading over the wicked.
Mournful praises
Shall be my reward.
Jah is always guiding.

The union representative handling my appeal—I've been begging him to file a discrimination claim with solicitors. He keeps telling me to get statements from others, but I'm the one being discriminated against. Let me list it:

Sausage Union *By Palmwine Sounds*

Discrimination

Privacy breach - Discrimination.
Selective investigation - Discrimination.
Targeting me - Discrimination.
Threats - Discrimination.
Hiding files - Discrimination.
Protected act breach - Discrimination.
Burying evidence - Discrimination.
Belief threats - Discrimination.
Racism - Discrimination.
Outcasting - Discrimination.
Ignorance - Discrimination.

I've spoken to countless solicitors. They all say my case is strong, and the union should handle it. What am I paying my union fees for? You are a trade union, not the warehouse's trade union. If you're working together, I will file my claim against both the union and the warehouse myself. I have three years. Even if I don't win, it will shine a light on the injustices going on in the warehouse.

Sausage Union
By Palmwine Sounds

Babylon only understands violence, and I shall give them.

Legal Violence

Where opportunities present,
Legal violence is sweeter.
The quill and ink become weapons,
And the law is my ammunition.

I pleaded with the union to do the needful. Would it not be beneficial to the union, bringing more trust from its members?

www.ingramcontent.com/pod-product-compliance
Lightning Source LLC
Chambersburg PA
CBHW060035180426
43196CB00045B/2694